Musical Gematria

William Zeitler

Musica Arcana :: San Bernardino, CA :: 2013

Musical Gematria

ISBN 978-1-940630-02-1

Printed in the U.S.A.

Musica Arcana
San Bernardino, CA
www.MusicaArcana.com

Contents

Introduction

'Gematria' is concerned with relating words to numbers, and words to each other through their numerical values. Gematria was most famously employed by the Cabalists — Jewish mystics of the Middle Ages and Renaissance — using the Hebrew Bible to mystically relate Hebrew words to each other (such as the names of God) by their numerical equivalence. The Greeks also used gematria along similar lines.

I have spent many decades searching for a way of doing 'musical gematria'. I have always found gematria intriguing; especially since I've taught mathematics at the college level, and I have an abiding interest in Biblical languages (I did my own translation of the New Testament from the original Greek into English). Being a musician since age 5 (and that has been my primary career for over three decades now) I have been intrigued with the idea of extending gematria — of word/number — to music. After all, music already has a profoundly mathematical and mystical character.

The vague idea of 'musical gematria' is one thing, realizing that in a concrete method of actually doing it is quite another. Every method of doing 'musical gematria' that I have tried over the years resulted in ugly musical chaos — that is (as I liked to put it): 'tone rows' à la Schoenberg and friends. No thank you![1]

(Some of my earlier attempts at 'Musical Gematria' can be found in my *Music of the Spheres* album (2003), in which primitive ideas of musical gematria found limited use in generating rhythmic, not melodic or harmonic, ideas.)

Meanwhile, it has always seemed to me that one of the inviolable criteria of a true Musical Gematria is that it results in musical gestures that are graceful. After all, according to Plato and many others since him, one of our 'primary values' is Beauty (the other two being Truth and Goodness (ethics)). Furthermore, it has always seemed to me that another criterion of a true/beautiful/good method of musical gematria is it be fundamentally simple and 'elegant'.

Imagine my surprise when, after over a decade of trying idea after idea that only resulted in the dreaded 'tone rows', I awoke one morning in November 2011 knowing how to do it. And not just one method — a whole family of approaches.

To explain musical gematria I have to explain gematria itself — which necessitates reviewing how the ancient Greeks and Hebrews expressed numbers. And it requires me to review some basic mathematics to which you were almost certainly exposed in grade school, but you have long forgotten because it has no general practical application. And it requires using the barest rudiments of musical notation. The historical surveys in this little book are highly superficial — just enough to present the principles of gematria — endnotes and the bibliography will guide interested readers to more details. Ultimately this little book is more concerned with introducing *musical* gematria to others who may use and develop it, and not with producing a scholarly work on gematria *per se*.

Grace and peace,

William Zeitler
October, 2013
San Bernardino, CA

Traditional Gematria

Pythagoras

Pythagoras (c.570–c.495 BCE) was a philosopher/mathematician/mystic. His students were sworn to secrecy, his teachings only shared later by Plato (427–347 BCE)[2] and others, so it is impossible at this point to know which ideas were Pythagoras' and those of his school.

That being said, the Pythagorean School taught that Number was the basis of everything:

> "The eternal being of [N]umber is a most provident principle of the whole heaven, earth, and of the intermediate nature; moreover it is a source of permanence for divine (men) and gods and daemons."[3]
> "All things are like unto [N]umber."[4]
> "Nothing whatever can be thought or known without Number."[5]

Because Number represents a celestial power working in the divine sphere, it is really a blueprint of creation. Number is itself divine and associated with the divinities.

Pythagorean ideas became an important thread in subsequent Greek philosophy.

Harmony

The Pythagorean School is credited with discovering the mathematical nature of harmonious musical note combinations. These ideas are most easily illustrated with a 'monochord' (a favorite tool of the Pythagoreans) — which is something like a one-stringed guitar:

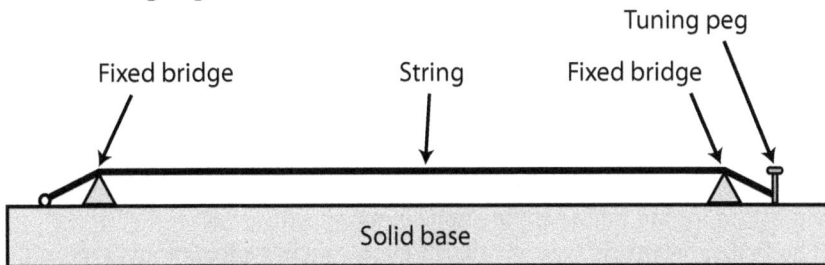

'Monochord' means 'one string' — you pluck the one string and get the one note. The two 'fixed bridges' — one on each end — determine the length of the vibrating string, which in turn determine the pitch.[6]

One note alone is hardly useful, so the monochord really comes into its own by adding one more bridge, a 'moveable bridge', which divides our single string into two parts:

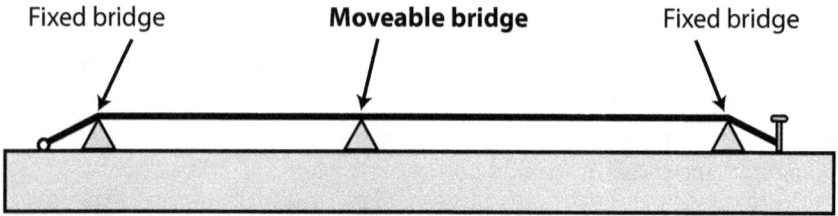

Fixed bridge   **Moveable bridge**   Fixed bridge

The 'moveable bridge' divides our string into two playable segments. If we pluck the string segment on the left of the moveable bridge, we'll get one pitch; if we pluck the string segment on the right, we'll get another (unless we place the moveable bridge exactly in the middle, in which case both string segments will sound the same pitch.)

We can put the moveable bridge anywhere we want. But suppose we put it at arithmetically special/simple positions:

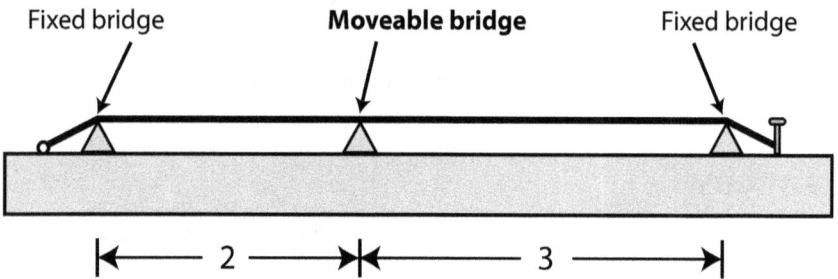

Fixed bridge   **Moveable bridge**   Fixed bridge

|← 2 →|← 3 →|

In this example, the string length on the left has a length of 2 relative to the string length on the right of 3. (It doesn't matter if we're using inches, centimeters, furlongs or light-years — the essential thing is the ratio of the two string lengths.) In this example, if we pluck the string segment on the left and then the string segment on the right, we will hear the pitches DO to SO — that is, DO [re me fa] SO. If you count DO=1, RE=2, MI=3, FA=4, SO=5, then 'SO' is the fifth step of DO-RE-MI..., and is known as the Perfect Fifth, one of the most important pitch combinations in music worldwide.

The Pythagoreans showed that harmonious pitch combinations (such as DO to SO) correspond to arithmetically simple string length ratios, such as 1 to 2, 2 to 3, 3 to 5, and so forth. (If the two string segments are close to "2 to 3" but not exact, they still sound musically harmonious because the ear is accustomed to imperfection. But diverging too far from simple ratios results in 'disharmony' or 'dissonance'.)

Thanks to modern physics we now understand that sound is the result of vibrations of air pushing and pulling the eardrum. The more of these vibrations per second, the higher the note. We now know that the ratios of string lengths correspond to the ratio of vibrations per second. And consequently the ratio of string lengths has the same effect as the ratios of vibrations of air per second: if the ratio of string lengths is 1:2, then the ratio of vibrations per second will be 2:1.

Music of the Spheres

The Pythagoreans extended this idea of harmony to the celestial planets. In a theory known as the 'Music of the Spheres' or 'Harmony of the Spheres' Pythagoras proposed that the Sun, Moon and planets all emit their own unique hum based on their orbital revolution. These celestial sounds are imperceptible to the human ear — in the same way that someone living next to a waterfall ceases to hear it after long acclimation.

Subsequently, Plato described astronomy and music as "twinned" studies of sensual recognition: astronomy for the eyes, music for the ears, both of which require knowledge of numerical proportions:

> As the eyes are framed for astronomy so the ears are framed for harmony: and these are in some form kindred sciences, as the Pythagoreans affirm and we admit.[7]

The idea of the 'harmony of the spheres' was important in Western astrology/astronomy until Kepler (1571-1630). Kepler's three mathematical laws of planetary motion are the beginnings of modern astrophysics — they are still taught in Physics 101. But, for example, his book *Harmony of the World* in which he introduces one of his famous laws, is a marvelous mixture of mathematical and musical notation.

Greek Gematria

In the modern Western world we are accustomed to having one set of characters for writing words ('A'/'a' through 'Z'/'z'), and another set of characters for writing numbers ('0' through '9'). This has not always been so. The ancient Greeks (and others) used their alphabet for both words *and* numbers. One result of this is that their words looked like strange numbers, and their numbers looked like strange words.

In other words, A–Θ represented 1–9, I–ϟ represented 10–90, and P–ϡ represented 100–900.[8] Thus, in this system, "ΧΟΗ" ("choē"), which means "a drink offering to the gods," has a numerical value of:

$$
\begin{aligned}
\text{X (ch)} &= 600 \\
\text{O (o)} &= 70 \\
\text{H (ē)} &= 8 \\
\hline
\text{Total} &= 678
\end{aligned}
$$

Remember, the Greeks weren't 'translating' their letters into numerals and then adding them. "XOH" was how they would normally write "678".[9]

Some say the Greeks adopted this system from the Phoenicians.[10] Others say that the Greeks invented it themselves.[11] Either way, you can see that to an ancient Greek the line between numbers and words was very thin indeed.

So one shouldn't be too surprised that the Greeks would use the gematria values of the names of their gods in the construction of their temples. In fact, the word 'gematria' itself argues for its use in the geometry of architecture, as the etymology of 'gematria' is that it was derived from the Greek word "geometria" ("earth-measures") from which we also get the word 'geometry'.[14]

In the Parthenon itself (to just name one example), the following dimensions appear — which also happen to be the gematria value of the indicated god[15]:

353	'Hermes'
318	'Helios' (the Sun)
612	'Zeus'
707	'The God Hermes'

(using the ancient Greek 'foot' as the
unit of measure)

By the way, applying gematria to their architecture wasn't unique to the Greeks: a Babylonian clay table indicates that around 700 BCE, Sargon II ordered that the wall of Khorsabad be constructed to have a length of 16,283 cubits, the numerical value of his name.[16]

Greek gematria all but disappeared from use with the general demise of Graeco-Roman culture in the Middle Ages.

	Greek Alphabet Table		
Letter[12]	Ancient Numerical Value	Letter Name	Transliteration
A α	1	Alpha	A
B β	2	Beta	B
Γ γ	3	Gamma	G
Δ δ	4	Delta	D
E ε	5	Epsilon	E
Ft ϝ*	6	Digamma (later Stigma)	St
Z ζ	7	Zeta	Z
H η	8	Eta	Ē
Θ θ	9	Theta	Th
I ι	10	Iota	I
K κ	20	Kappa	K
Λ λ	30	Lamda	L
M μ	40	Mu	M
N ν	50	Nu	N
Ξ ξ	60	Xi	X
O o	70	Omicron	O
Π π	80	Pi	P
Ϙ ϙ*	90	Koppa	Q
P ρ	100	Rho	R
Σ σ ς	200	Sigma	S
T τ	300	Tau	T
Y υ	400	Upsilon	Y/U
Φ φ	500	Phi	Ph
X χ	600	Chi	Ch
Ψ ψ	700	Psi	Ps
Ω ω	800	Omega	Ō
Ϡ ϡ*	900	Sampi	ts?

*Archaic[13]

8

Hebrew Gematria

By around the first through sixth centuries CE, the Hebrews were using an alphabetic numbering similar to that of the Greeks:

Hebrew Alphabet Table			
Letter	Numerical Value	Letter Name	Transliteration
א	1	Alef	A
ב	2	Bet	B
ג	3	Gimel	G
ד	4	Dalet	D
ה	5	He	H
ו	6	Vav	W/V
ז	7	Zayin	Z
ח	8	Het	Ch (as in "Bach" and "Loch")
ט	9	Tet	T
י	10	Yod	Y
כ/ך	20	Kaf	K
ל	30	Lamed	L
מ/ם	40	Mem	M
נ/ן	50	Nun	N
ס	60	Samekh	S
ע	70	Ayin	-
פ/ף	80	Pe	P
צ/ץ	90	Tsadi	Ts
ק	100	Qof	Q
ר	200	Resh	R
ש	300	Shin	s/sh
ת	400	Tav	T

Hundreds greater than 400 were represented by the sum of two or more letters representing hundreds.[17]

Apparently the Hebrews learned the numerical use of the alphabet from the Greeks.[18] Wherever they learned it, it would certainly be true that the line between a number and a word was very thin to the ancient Hebrews, and it would be easy and natural to view a word as an odd looking number and vice versa.[19]

Hebrew gematria was taken to heart and greatly developed by medieval and Renaissance Jewish mystics in a field of study known as 'Kabbalah'.[20] In their way of thinking, the gematria values of the names of G-d were thought to reveal characteristics of G-d.[21]

Latin Gematria

The Romans may not have been interested in gematria, but medieval and Renaissance (esoteric) Christians were. And Latin was the universal language of the educated for approximately a millennium. Here is a fairly standard table for Latin gematria:[22]

Latin Alphabet Table	
Letter	Numerical Value
A	1
B	2
C	3
D	4
E	5
F	6
G	7
H	8
I	9
K	10
L	20
M	30
N	40
O	50
P	60
Q	70
R	80
S	90
T	100
U	200
X	300
Y	400
Z	500

English Gematria

In modern English the customary way of relating the counting numbers to the letters of the alphabet is to use 'simple enumeration' (number them successively): Modern numerology makes much of the sum of the simple enumeration of the letters in a name. ("Simple enumeration" being 'A' = 1, 'B' = 2, ... 'Z' = 26).

English Alphabet Table	
Letter	Simple Enumeration
A	1
B	2
C	3
D	4
E	5
F	6
G	7
H	8
I	9
J	10
K	11
L	12
M	13
N	14
O	15
P	16
Q	17
R	18
S	19
T	20
U	21
V	22
W	23
X	24
Y	25
Z	26

Other Ancient Numbering Systems

Implicit in the ancient Greek and Hebrew numbering systems is grouping by ten: one set of characters for the numbers 1–9, another for the numbers 10–90, etc.

Now, grouping and numbering by tens is entirely natural for us humans, as we have 10 fingers to use as digits. In fact, another name for 'finger' is 'digit'. But grouping and numbering by tens was certainly not universal. Greenlanders counted by twenties (using both fingers and toes), as did the Aztecs, and the Mayans (for the most part). And the ancient Sumerians counted by 60s for astronomical observations (but by tens for everyday use) — we still see the vestiges of that in '60 minutes to an hour'.

And of course there were yet other ways of representing numbers in the ancient world, such as Roman numerals.

Number Bases

Mathematics in more modern times has shown that basing our numbers on '10' is far from the only option.

Imagine the odometer on a car. It starts out at:

$$\boxed{0}\boxed{0}\boxed{0}\boxed{0}\boxed{0}\boxed{0}$$

As you drive it, the right most 'wheel' of the odometer (well, they used to be real wheels until they were replaced by electronics) advances to 1, then 2, etc. until it gets to 9:

$$\boxed{0}\boxed{0}\boxed{0}\boxed{0}\boxed{0}\boxed{9}$$

Then the right-most wheel turns to 0, and the wheel just to its left advances to 1:

$$\boxed{0}\boxed{0}\boxed{0}\boxed{0}\boxed{1}\boxed{0}$$

As we continue to drive the car, the right-most wheel will eventually advance to 9 again:

$$\boxed{0}\boxed{0}\boxed{0}\boxed{0}\boxed{1}\boxed{9}$$

When the right-most wheel advances to 0, the wheel to its immediate left advances again:

$$\boxed{0}\boxed{0}\boxed{0}\boxed{0}\boxed{2}\boxed{0}$$

Eventually both wheels will advance to 9:

$$\boxed{0}\boxed{0}\boxed{0}\boxed{0}\boxed{9}\boxed{9}$$

Driving one more mile (or kilometer) causes the right most wheel to advance from 9 to 0, which means that the wheel to its left must advance by one. But that wheel is at 9 also, so it also advances from 9 to 0, and the wheel to *its* left advances to 1 as well:

$$\boxed{0}\boxed{0}\boxed{0}\boxed{1}\boxed{0}\boxed{0}$$

This is how we count in the modern West, and it is called a 'positional' numbering system, because the quantity represented by a digit is determined by its position. The right-most wheel always represents how many 1's. Furthermore, we say this is 'base 10', because each of our wheels has 10 digits on it. And to figure out what the wheel to the immediate left of any wheel represents, you multiply by 10.

We could just as easily use odometer wheels that had only eight digits: 0

through 7. Once again, we begin at:

0	0	0	0	0	0

Then we start driving....

0	0	0	0	0	7

But we have no more digits after '7', so that wheel advances to '0' and the wheel to its left advances by one:

0	0	0	0	1	0

etc....

0	0	0	0	1	7

0	0	0	0	2	0

etc....

0	0	0	0	7	7

0	0	0	1	0	0

The smallest number of digits you can have and still be able to count is 2, and our two and only two digits will be '0' and '1'. Counting in base 2 looks like this:

0	0	0	0	0	0

0	0	0	0	0	1

But we don't have any more digits after 1. So that wheel advances to 0 and we increment the next wheel to the left...

0	0	0	0	1	0

0	0	0	0	1	1

0	0	0	1	0	0

0	0	0	1	0	1

0	0	0	1	1	0

∞ Musical Gematria ∞

0	0	0	1	1	1

0	0	1	0	0	0

This may seem like a crazy way to count, but it turns out that base 2 is enormously useful. The very first computers were designed to use base 10 internally, just like their human designers. But this didn't work — the electronics turned out to be too cumbersome and error prone. They ultimately decided to use base 2, because a base 2 electronic device is vastly more reliable, and so simple it can be made economically by the millions — and the computer revolution was born.

By the way, when writing numbers instead of looking at them on odometers, we customarily leave off all the 'leading zeros' — '100' is a lot easier to read than '000100' and the leading zeros don't tell us anything. Also, in contexts where there is any question about which base we are using, we can write a subscript indicating the base after the number:

$$1000_2 \quad \text{is 1000 base 2}$$
$$124_8 \quad \text{is 124 base 8}$$

To summarize, we have seen that our modern base 10 system of notating numbers may be practical, but others are equally valid and may be more suitable for some purposes. That is, although base 10 works well for most human applications — and we have a bias towards base 10 because we have 10 fingers — there may be situations where some other number base may work better.

For example, the number '7' has all sorts of mystical importance. So for certain mystical purposes, it might make more sense to use base 7 than base 10.

After all, to limit ourselves to just base 10 is like a painter limiting themselves to just the one color, or a musician to just one key.

Music and Gematria

Music and Number Bases

Consider the notes of the 'DO, RE, MI' scale:

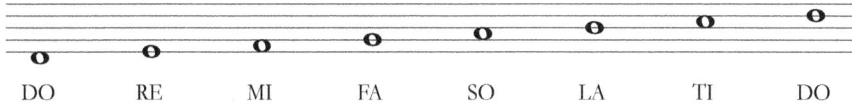

DO	RE	MI	FA	SO	LA	TI	DO

(If you don't know how to read music, here's all you need to know for this discussion: notice that each circle is centered on a line or space. As you go up "line, space, line, space", you are going up the "white notes" on the piano keyboard. So DO is on a space, RE is on the next line up, MI is on the next space up, and so on.)

From the lower DO to the upper DO is called an 'octave' — one of the most important note relationships in all music everywhere in the world. It has a basis in physics: the upper DO always vibrates at twice the vibrations per second of the lower DO. So if the lower DO is vibrating at, say, 100 vibrations per second, the 'upper' DO vibrates at twice that, namely 200 vibrations per second.[23] On a monochord, the string lengths would be in a ratio of 1 to 2.

As you continue up the scale, the pattern of DO, RE, MI repeats itself:

DO	RE	MI	FA	SO	LA	TI	DO	RE	MI	FA	etc...

The same pattern holds if you go *down* the scale (note: when you run out of lines for your "line, space, line, space", you just draw more short ones):

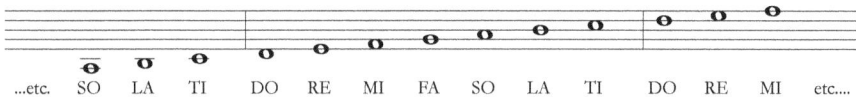

...etc.	SO	LA	TI	DO	RE	MI	FA	SO	LA	TI	DO	RE	MI	etc....

DO RE MI goes up infinitely (and down infinitely) making it a great spiral: as you ascend the scale, each DO circles back on itself but at exactly twice the vibration. (Our physical ears, however, are only capable of hearing about 10 octaves or so.)

By the way, the same 2 to 1 octave relationship holds not just for DO, but also for the rest of the notes of DO RE MI — if you go from the RE in one octave to the RE in the next octave higher, the higher RE vibrates exactly twice as fast as the lower RE. And so on.

The idea that 'DO' is still 'DO' regardless of the octave in which it occurs is known as '**octave equivalence**'.

Suppose we want to number the notes of our scale. We could do something

18

like this:

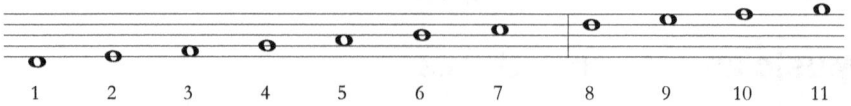

| 1 | 2 | 3 | 4 | 5 | 6 | 7 | 8 | 9 | 10 | 11 |

But notice that there are seven notes in DO RE MI before we get to the next DO and the pattern starts repeating itself again. What if we number the notes using base 7 (because there are 7 notes in our scale), and begin with 0 as in our odometer examples earlier:

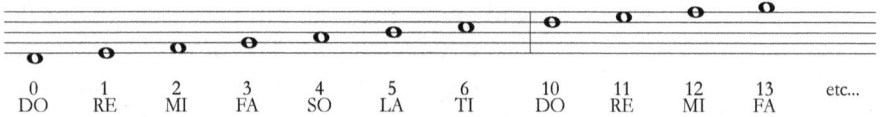

| 0 | 1 | 2 | 3 | 4 | 5 | 6 | 10 | 11 | 12 | 13 | etc... |
| DO | RE | MI | FA | SO | LA | TI | DO | RE | MI | FA | |

Notice that in the last digit (the 1's place), DO is always 0, RE is always 1, and so on. And the first digit (the 7's place) tells us how many octaves up we've gone. (In the first octave in this example, the '0' in the 7's place is implied — remember 'no leading zeros' in our earlier odometer examples.) So, counting our 7-note DO-RE-MI scale using base 7, these two rules always hold true:

- The right-most digit (the 1's place) indicates the note of the scale (e.g. DO is always 0), and
- The left-most digit (the 7's place) indicates the number of octaves up

Musical Gematria

As an aside, the first three centuries of Christianity were theologically the 'Wild West'. Opinions varied wildly on what are now accepted standard doctrines, such as 'the Trinity' and 'the Divinity of Christ'. (Contributing to the turmoil, Christians in those first few centuries could also be a little busy dealing with persecutions, being fed to the lions, and so on.) In this Christian cauldron were groups that were very interested in incorporating Greek ideas in general and Pythagoras in particular into the teachings of Jesus. So for some Christian groups in those first few centuries, gematria was a significant part of their belief systems. Then Constantine legalized Christianity in 313, becoming the first Christian Emperor (although opinions vary wildly as to just how devout he was in practice). Constantine was very interested in establishing what the 'one true official' Christianity should be, and convened Councils of Nicaea (held in Nicaea, found in what is now north-western Turkey) to establish the 'one true faith'. Other variants of Christianity that didn't get with the program were suppressed with the full authority and might of Rome. So anything resembling 'Pythagorean Christianity' disappeared (or went deeply underground) and with it gematria.

ᔛ Musical Gematria ᔜ

We are ready to do 'musical gematria', and in honor of those early forgotten Christian Pythagorean 'Gematrians', let's use the name 'Jesus', which in Greek was IĒSOUS ('Ιησοῦς).[24] By Greek gematria this has the value

$$\text{'Ιησοῦς (IĒSOUS)} = 10 + 8 + 200 + 70 + 400 + 200 = 888$$

In ancient gematria thinking, '8' is the number of renewal, new beginnings: a new week begins after eight days; after seven notes of the scale (DO-RE-MI) it begins again at DO — at the OCTave (OCT being the prefix for '8').

On the other hand the number of 'The Beast' in the Book of Revelation in the Bible is '666'.[25] ('6' is the number of 'humanity': e.g. humanity was created on the Sixth Day in Genesis 1.)

Now,

$$888_{10} = 2406_7$$

That is, 888 base 10 = 2406 base 7. Simply numbering DO RE MI, counting from 0 (and we are ignoring octaves for the moment), we have:

0	1	2	3	4	5	6
DO	RE	MI	FA	SO	LA	TI

'Rewriting' the digits of 2406_7 into their musical equivalents, we have:

2	4	0	6
MI	SO	DO	TI

By octave equivalence we can move TI down an octave (that is, TI will still be TI, regardless of its octave) to get a more graceful musical gesture if we want:

2	4	0	6
MI	SO	DO	TI

This was an example of how to do musical gematria for 'melody' — I suppose we could call it 'melodic gematria'. It remains to give examples of how one might do musical gematria using the other basic aspects of music, namely 'rhythm' and 'harmony'. Because they are more complex, I've consigned them to the end as 'examples'.

∽ William Zeitler ∾

In summary, the key idea is to use the number base that best fits the situation instead of automatically limiting oneself to just base 10. (If we have 7 notes in a scale, why not consider using base 7?)

A constant self-limiting habit of human beings is that we are habitually anthropocentric (WE are the center of Life, the Universe and Everything) and we constantly anthropomorphize (projecting human behaviors onto everything and everyone). The only reason we use base 10 is because we have 10 fingers. Consequently we count in base 10, and our approach to number is dominated by that cognitive filter.

So the approach to musical gematria described herein amounts to relaxing the vice grip of our habitual anthropocentric and anthropomorphic base 10 way of thinking numerically.

The Significance of Musical Gematria

We saw how the relationship between the Cosmos and Number was very close for the Pythagoreans. We saw how the Pythagoreans were particularly interested in vibrating strings and their mathematical properties.

In modern physics, the current frontrunner theory of 'what everything is made of' is known as 'string theory' because it is based on the same fundamental mathematics as that of vibrating strings.[26] Thus, according to string theory, the basic building blocks of the Cosmos amount to infinitesimally small monochords! Maybe Pythagoras was more prescient than anyone could have guessed! In any event, modern physics is arguably the full flowering of Pythagoras idea that the Cosmos is governed by number.

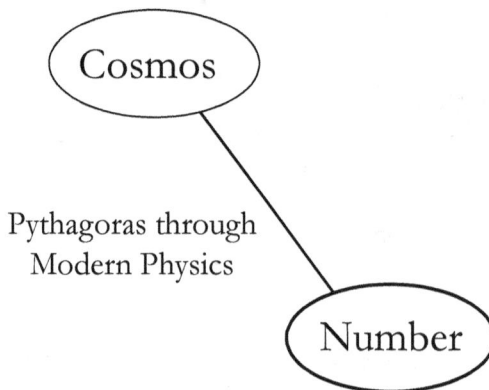

Cosmos

Pythagoras through
Modern Physics

Number

As Betrand Russell noted: "Perhaps the oddest thing about Modern Science is its return to Pythagoreanism."[27]

We also saw how the ancient Greeks and Hebrews[28] used the letters of their alphabet both as letters and as digits, so the veil between 'words' and 'numbers' was very thin. We saw how investigation into the relationships of words and numbers is called 'gematria':

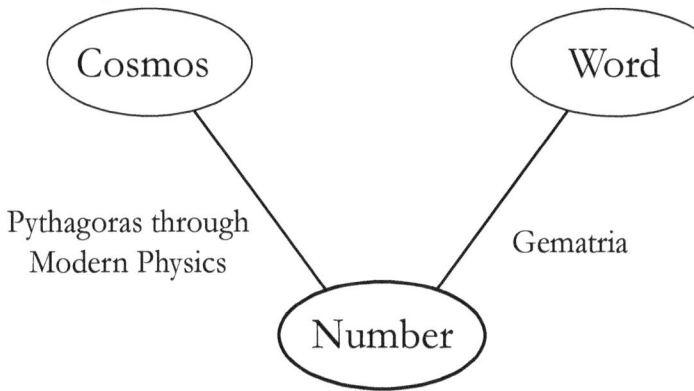

We also saw how the Greeks apparently used the gematria values of divine names as dimensions in their temples. The term 'sacred geometry' refers to the use of geometry in the design of sacred spaces — the gematria of divine names applied to the geometry of sacred spaces would seem to fall under that heading.

And if the Greeks used gematria in the design of buildings, might they have used it in their sculptures and other art works? After all, they applied sophisticated geometry to their visual arts.[29]

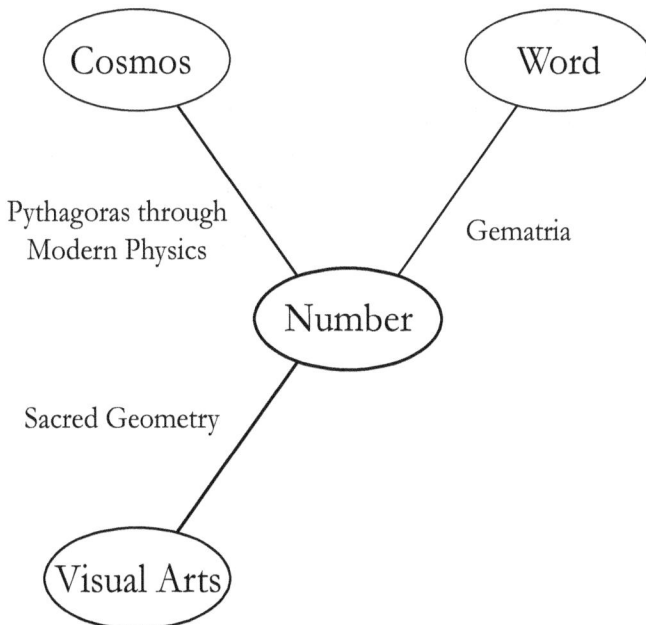

∽ William Zeitler ∾

Finally, with 'musical gematria', we are able to integrate not just pitch ratios on a monochord, but Music itself into Pythagoras' Grand Number Theory:

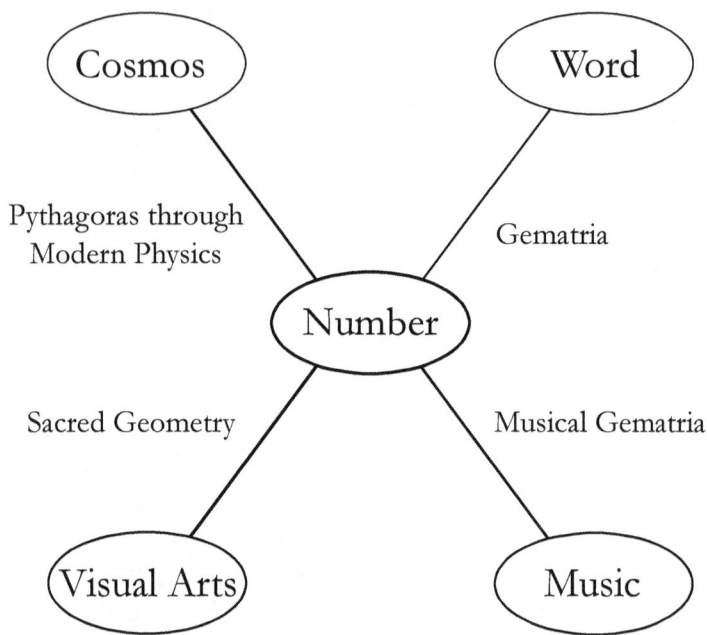

The concept behind this diagram is hardly new. Plato himself said much the same thing:

> **Every [geometric] diagram, and system of number, and every combination of harmony, and the agreement of the revolution of the stars** must be manifest as One through All to him who learns in the proper way. And [they] will disclose themselves if, as we say, a man learns aright by keeping his gaze on Unity; for it will be manifest to us, as we reflect, that there is one bond naturally uniting all these things.
> – Plato, *Epinomis*[30] [emphasis added]

Examples

Example 1: Melodic Musical Gematria

Since I've given a Greek musical gematria example ('Jesus' IĒSOUS), it seemed like a Hebrew example is also in order. Considering that 'Song of Songs' is presumably a song, that seemed like a likely candidate for generating a melodic gesture. I've chosen:

אני חבצלת השרון

"I am the rose of Sharon." (Song of Songs 2:1)

In Hebrew writing at the time this was written (and until the 1st millennium) words were not separated by spaces. Consequently for purposes of musical gematria, it seems to me best to use the gematria sum of this entire phrase (as opposed to sums on each of the words separately).

So, we have (reading right to left):

א (A)	=	1
נ (N)	=	50
י (Y)	=	10
ח (Ch)	=	8
ב (B)	=	2
צ (Ts)	=	90
ל (L)	=	30
ת (T)	=	400
ה (H)	=	5
ש (S)	=	300
ר R	=	200
ו (W)	=	6
ן (N)	=	50

TOTAL $= 1152_{10}$ / 3234_7

Using our same base 7 numbering of DO-RE-MI as we used above, we have:

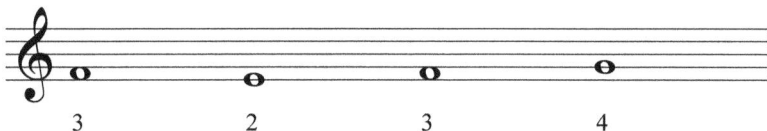

3   2   3   4

∾ William Zeitler ∾

Example 2: Rhythmic Musical Gematria

Let's begin by expressing the word IĒSOUS in base 2 ('binary') gematria:

$$IĒSOUS = 1101111000_2$$

Since we're interested in rhythm, let's play this on a drum. Reading left to right let each '1' indicate a drum hit, and each '0' a rest:

$$1 \quad 1 \quad 0 \quad 1 \quad 1 \quad 1 \quad 1 \quad 0 \quad 0 \quad 0$$

If we have two drums, say 'high' and 'low', we could use base 4:

$$IĒSOUS = 31320_4$$

We use base 4 because with two drums we have 4 different ways of combining them:[31]

0	Rest / silence / neither drum
1	High drum only
2	Low drum only
3	High and low drum

Which gives us:

In general it seems natural to let '0' represent silence / a rest / neither drum. Using '0' to represent silence has the additional advantage that any rhythmic gematria will always have something happening (a non-rest) on the down beat.[32]

Example 3: Harmonic Musical Gematria

'Magic squares' are squares in which each row, column and diagonal adds up to the same sum. They aren't easy to come by. Here's one:

11	24	7	20	3
4	12	25	8	16
17	5	13	21	9
10	18	1	14	22
23	6	19	2	15

In this magic square above, each row, column and diagonal adds up to 65. If we assign a note to each row and each column, we have:

	C	D	E	F	G
C	11	24	7	20	3
D	4	12	25	8	16
E	17	5	13	21	9
F	10	18	1	14	22
G	23	6	19	2	15

If we assign the successive letters of the Greek alphabet to the counting numbers ('simple enumeration'), so A = 1, B = 2, Γ = 3 … Ω = 24:

	C	**D**	**E**	**F**	**G**
C	Λ	Ω	H	Υ	Γ
D	Δ	M	~	Θ	Π
E	P	E	N	Φ	I
F	K	Σ	A	Ξ	X
G	Ψ	Z	T	B	O

('~' = no letter assigned.)

So IĒSOUS gives us these note pairs (row, column):

I (I)	G, E
H (Ē)	E, C
Σ (S)	D, F
O (O)	G, G
Υ (U)	F, C
Σ (S)	D, F

Or:

I   H   Σ   O   Y   Σ

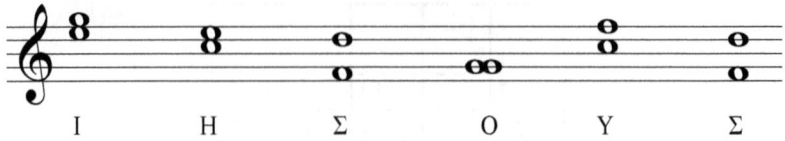

If a 2-dimensional magic square gives us 2 notes at a time, a 3-dimensional magic cube will give us 3 notes at a time.[33] Here's an example of a 3x3x3 magic cube (each up/down, right/left, and in/out adds up to 42.):

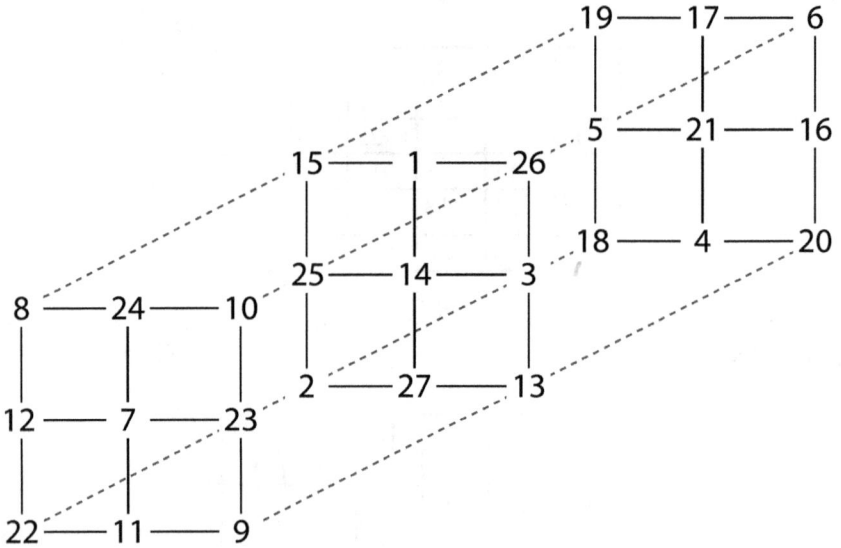

```
                                    19 ——— 17 ——— 6
                                    |      |      |
                                    5 ——— 21 ——— 16
                15 ——— 1 ——— 26     |      |      |
                |      |      |     18 ——— 4 ——— 20
                25 ——— 14 ——— 3
  8 ——— 24 ——— 10   |     |     |
  |      |      |    2 ——— 27 ——— 13
 12 ——— 7 ——— 23
  |      |      |
 22 ——— 11 ——— 9
```

If we replace the numbers with the simple enumeration of the Greek alphabet we will have:

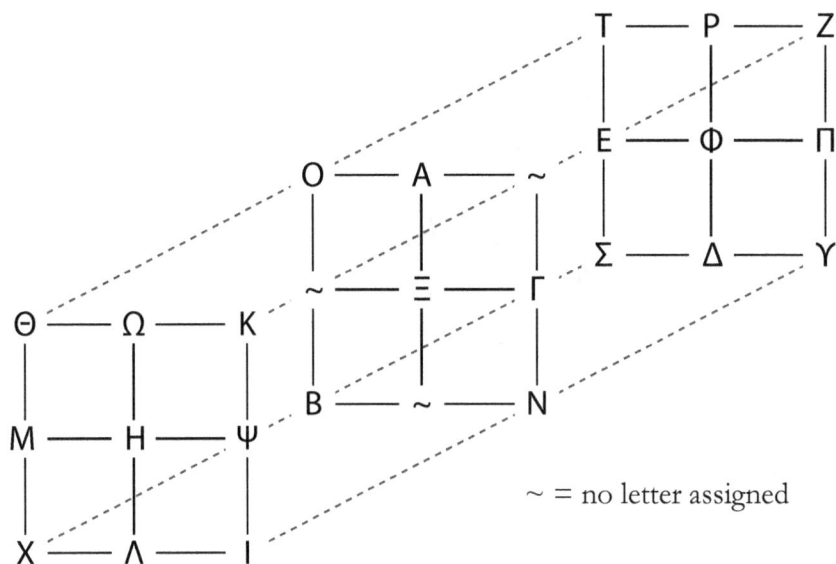

~ = no letter assigned

Suppose we use a 9-note scale,[34] namely, the 'Aerycrygic ("air-ih-KRI-jik) mode':[35]

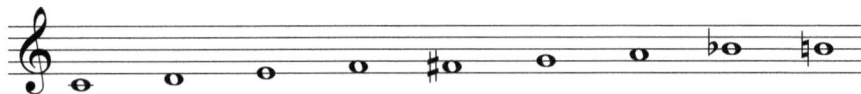

Because we have 3 up/down rows, 3 right/left columns, and 3 in/out layers, we can assign the 3 + 3 + 3 notes of the Aerycrygic mode to our rows/columns/layers:

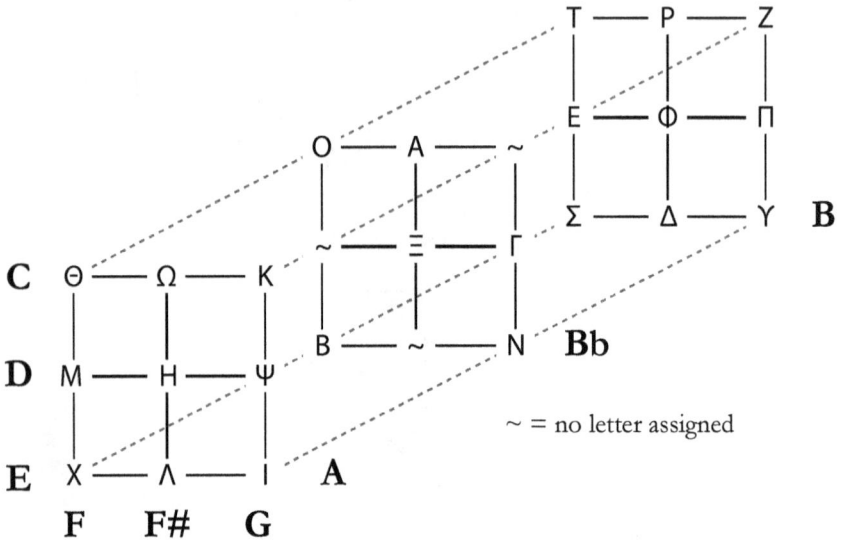

~ = no letter assigned

Thus, if we take the letter 'I', we see that it corresponds to up/down position 'E', and left/right position 'G', and in/out position 'A'.

Continuing that process with all the letters of 'IĒSOUS', we have:

	Up/down	Right/left	In/out
I (I)	E	G	A
H (Ē)	D	F#	A
Σ (S)	E	F	B
O (O)	C	F	Bb
Υ (U)	E	G	B
Σ (S)	E	F	B

Or:

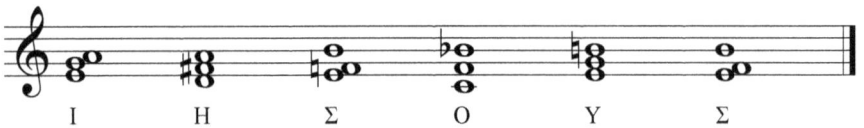

I   H   Σ   O   Υ   Σ

Example 4: 'B-A-C-H'

This example is not gematria proper, but it's eerily close.

There are seven white keys per octave on the piano, and most of the West uses the seven letters 'A' through 'G' to name them. But Northern Europe used a slightly different system (still in use today):

Generally	Northern Europe
A	A
Bb	**B**
B	**H**
C	C
D	D
E	E
F	F
G	G

The famous composer Johann Sebastian Bach (1685-1750) lived in northern Europe, and thus it was natural for him to musically express his last name using the note letters in common use in his region:

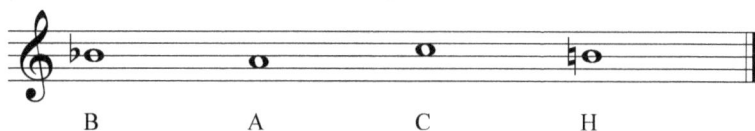

B   A   C   H

And he did just that in the last fugue of his epic *Art of Fugue*, composed at the end of his life. (Sadly he didn't live to complete it.)

In honor of Bach, other composers have written music on the name B-A-C-H (fugues mostly — Bach's specialty). In a comprehensive study published in the catalogue for the 1985 exhibition "300 Jahre Johann Sebastian Bach" ("300 years of Johann Sebastian Bach") in Stuttgart, Germany, Ulrich Prinz lists 409 works by 330 composers from the 17th to the 20th century using the B-A-C-H motif.[36] Here are a few:

1845 - Robert Schumann: *Six Fugues on the Name: BACH* Op. 60
1855 - Franz Liszt: *Fantasy and Fugue on the Theme B-A-C-H*, for organ
1856 - Johannes Brahms: *Fugue in A-flat minor* for organ, WoO 8[7]
1878 - Nikolai Rimsky-Korsakov: *Variations on BACH*, for piano
1900 - Max Reger: *Fantasia and Fugue on B-A-C-H* for organ
1910 - Ferruccio Busoni: *Fantasia contrappuntistica* for piano
1926-28 - Arnold Schoenberg: *Variations for Orchestra*, Op. 31[9]
1932 - Francis Poulenc: *Valse-improvisation sur le nom Bach* for piano
1937-38 - Anton Webern: *String Quartet* (the tone row is based on the BACH motif)
1964 - Arvo Pärt: *Collage over B-A-C-H* for strings, oboe, harpsichord and piano

Bach's name has been expressed as a 'musical cross' (although not by Bach himself as far as we know). Starting with the left hand arm and proceeding clockwise yields B-A-C-H.[37]

Other methods of representing other names with music have been used down through the ages, although none as elegant, simple and natural as Bach's own name, using the standard note nomenclature of his day and region.[38] Not even the musical gematria presented in this monograph is anywhere nearly as elegant!

Notes

1. Not 'tone rows' strictly speaking, of course, but sharing that utterly anti-tonal character.

   It must be pointed out that attempts were made at something like 'musical gematria' in the first half of the 18th century at least in Germany by contemporaries of Bach. None of these proposed systems was found to be very satisfactory — in part (I think) because they weren't flexible enough to yield graceful musical gestures, and also because all interest in such things was a general casualty of the Enlightenment which was beginning to take hold at that time. See Tatlow, *Bach and the Riddle of the Number Alphabet*

2. In fact, McClain in *The Pythagorean Plato* argues that Plato's *Republic* is not only a tome on political theory but also an enormous musical metaphor.

3. Iamblichus, *On the Pythagorean Way of Life*, p.165

4. Ibid p.177

5. Laertius, *The Fragments of Philolaus*, quoted from Guthrie, *The Pythagorean Sourcebook* p.168

6. In addition to length, the pitch of a string is also determined by the string's tension, diameter and the stiffness of the material of which the string is made.

7. Plato, *Republic* VII.XII/p.189

8. Additional marks indicated that these should multiplied these by 1000 so larger numbers could be represented. At the same time, in an agrarian society, how large of numbers would you actually need in general practice?

9. The Greeks frequently used additional marks to ensure that numbers were not confused with text. See Ifrah, *From One To Zero*, 261ff.

10. Barry, *The Greek Qabalah*, p. 7ff; Fideler, *Jesus Christ, Sun of God*, p.26; Gullberg, *Mathematics: From the Birth of Numbers*, p.10ff.; Menninger & Broneer. *Number Words and Number Symbols a Cultural History of Numbers*, p.262

11. Ifrah, *From One To Zero*, p.275ff

12. The lower case Greek letters weren't in use this early, they are provided in the table only for reference.

13. For further information on these archaic forms, see the entries for the letters in Liddell & Scott, *A Greek-English Lexicon*

14. See the entry on 'gematria' in Trumble & Brown, *Shorter Oxford English Dictionary*

15. Fideler, *Jesus Christ, Sun of God*, 216-219

16. Contenau, *Everyday Life in Babylon and Assyria*, p.166

17. Certain Hebrew letters have more than one form — the form to the right is used at the end of words. Some versions of Hebrew gematria assign values greater than 400 to these final forms.

18. Ifrah, From *One To Zero*, p.270; Menninger & Broneer. *Number Words and Number Symbols*, pp. 264-5; Gullberg, *Mathematics: From the Birth of Numbers*, p.38

19. The Hebrews had their own system of additional marks to make sure numbers were correctly identified as numbers. See Ifrah, *From One To Zero*, 251ff

20. 'Gematria' was a very small part of the larger system of Kabbalah. See *Kabbalah*, Scholem

∾ William Zeitler ∾

21. To many of these Jewish mystics, and indeed still today in certain branches of Judaism, the names of God are so holy that even the word "G-O-D" is not to be written out. Hence the usage 'G-d'.
22. Agrippa, *Three Books of Occult Philosophy* (1532), Book II: chapter xx.
23. Due to a phenomenon called 'inharmonicity' in real-world stringed instruments, octaves are sometimes 'stretched' a tiny amount greater than an exact 1:2 ratio to sound better.
24. Thanks to Alexander the Great (336-323 BCE) who spread Greek language and culture throughout his empire, Greek became a common 'second language' in the ancient Mediterranean world. Greek was certainly a common language in the crossroads that was first century Palestine, and it seems entirely possible that Jesus was at least bilingual, speaking both Greek and Aramaic, and using whatever made the most sense for the audience at hand. Meanwhile, some scholars insist Jesus only spoke Greek, others that he only spoke Aramaic. In any event, the Greek gematria value of IĒSOUS (Ἰησοῦς) was used by early Christians — see Fideler, *Jesus Christ, Sun of God* and Berry, *Greek Qabalah*.
25. Rev.13:18. Ancient New Testament manuscripts disagree on this point, however: the number of The Beast could be 616 instead — see the apparatus for Rev.13:18 in Nestle et al, *Biblia Sacra*. For an in-depth investigation into gematria and numerology in the Bible, see Bullinger, *Number in Scripture*.
26. Greene, *The Elegant Universe* is a fascinating and reader-friendly introduction to string theory.
27. Quoted in Ghyka, *The Geometry of Art and Life*, p.168
28. Gematria in the ancient world was by no means limited to just Greek and Hebrew. There was also Ethiopic and Coptic gematria, to name only two.
29. Ghyka, *The Geometry of Art and Life*, 133ff.
30. Plato, *Charmides, Alcibiades I and II, Hipparchus, The Lovers, Theages, Minos, Epinomis*, 991E-992/p.485
31. The reader may notice that this chart could be rewritten:

00_2	Rest/Silence/Neither Drum
01_2	High drum
10_2	Low drum
11_2	High + low drum

In other words, a 1 in the 1's place of our binary representation of the drums to strike indicates the high drum, and a 1 in the 10's place of our binary representation of the drums to strike indicates the low drum.

32. If we don't use leading-zeros, our rhythmic gematria will never begin with a '0'.
33. And a four-dimensional 'hypercube' would give us 4 notes at a time.
34. Seven note scales have a special place in Western music, especially the well-known "DO-RE-MI" scale (and its modes). But just as there is a place for non-base-10 numbers, there is also a place for non-7-note scales. The 'whole-tone' and 'diminished' scales would be examples of non-7-note scales already in use in the West.

∽ Musical Gematria ∾

35.   The C major scale has no sharps or flats. The two scales with one accidental are G major (one sharp) and F major (one flat). It is no accident that G is a perfect 5th up from C, and F is a perfect 5th down from C. In G major the only note with an accidental is F#. In F major the only note with an accidental if Bb. The 'C Aerycrygic mode' is a merger of the C major, F major and G major scales. See http://www.AllTheScales.org.

36.   Bach, Prinz, and Küster, *300 Jahre Johann Sebastian Bach*

37.   With the 'C' clef 𝄡 , the point in the middle indicates middle C.

38.   See the Wikipedia articles on "Musical Cryptogram" and "Bach Motif"

Bibliography

Agrippa, Henry Cornelius (1533); *Three Books of Occult Philosophy*; Woodbury, MN. Llewellyn Publications, 2013

Bach, Johann Sebastian (1992). *The Art of the Fugue; and A Musical Offering*; Dover; New York

Bach, Johann Sebastian, Ulrich Prinz, and Konrad Küster (1985); *300 Jahre Johann Sebastian Bach: Sein Werk in Handschriften Und Dokumenten, Musikinstrumente Seiner Zeit, Seine Zeitgenossen : Eine Ausstellung Der Internationalen Bachakademie in Der Staatsgalerie Stuttgart, 14.9. Bis 27.10.1985*; H. Schneider; Tutzing

Barry, Kieren (1999); *The Greek Qabalah: Alphabetic Mysticism and Numerology in the Ancient World*; Samuel Weiser; York Beach, ME

Bond, Frederick Bligh and Lea, Thomas Simcox (1917); *Gematria (: A Preliminary Investigation of the Cabala Contained in the Coptic Gnostic Books and of a Similar Gematria in the Greek Text of the New Testament*. Research into Lost Knowledge Organization; London 1981

Bullinger, Ethelbert W. (1921); *Number in Scripture*; Martino; Mansfield Center, CT 2011

Contenau, Georges. *Everyday Life in Babylon and Assyria.*(1966); W.W. Norton; NY

Crane, Gregory, ed. *Perseus Digital Library*. *Perseus Digital Library*. Tufts University, 9 Mar. 2012. Web. 09 Mar. 2012. <http://www.perseus.tufts.edu>.

Daniels, Peter T., and William Bright (1996). *The World's Writing Systems*. Oxford University Press; New York

Dowling, Jay W., and Dane L. Harwood (1986); *Music Cognition*; Academic Press; San Diego

Fideler, David R. (1993); *Jesus Christ, Sun of God: Ancient Cosmology and Early Christian Symbolism*; Quest; Wheaton, IL

Ghyka, Matila C. (1977) *The Geometry of Art and Life*; Dover; New York

Godwin, Joscelyn (1993); *The Harmony of the Spheres: A Sourcebook of the Pythagorean Tradition in Music;* Inner Traditions International; Rochester, VT

Greene, B. (2003); *The Elegant Universe: Superstrings, Hidden Dimensions, and the Quest for the Ultimate Theory*; W.W. Norton; New York

Gullberg, Jan. (1997); *Mathematics: From the Birth of Numbers*; W.W. Norton; New York

Guthrie, Kenneth Sylvan., and David R. Fideler (1988) *The Pythagorean Sourcebook and Library: An Anthology of Ancient Writings Which Relate to Pythagoras and Pythagorean Philosophy;* Phanes; Grand Rapids

Iamblichus; *On the Pythagorean Way of Life*. Trans. John M. Dillon and Jackson P.

36

Hershbell; Scholars; Atlanta, GA 1991

Ifrah, Georges (1985); *From One To Zero*; Viking; NY

Kepler, Johannes. *The Harmony of the World*. Ed. E. J. Aiton, A. M. Duncan, and Judith Veronica Field;.American Philosophical Society; Philadelphia 1997

Liddell, Henry George, Robert Scott, Henry Stuart Jones, and Roderick McKenzie (1996); *A Greek-English Lexicon*; Clarendon; Oxford

McClain, Ernest G. (1984); *The Pythagorean Plato: Prelude to the Song Itself*; N. Hays; York Beach, ME

Menninger, Karl Augustus, and Paul Broneer (1970); *Number Words and Number Symbols a Cultural History of Numbers*; M.I.T; Cambridge

Michell, John F. (1973) *City of Revelation: On the Proportion and Symbolic Numbers of the Cosmic Temple*; Abacus; London

Nestle, Eberhard, Erwin Nestle, Kurt Aland, Rudolf Kittel, Karl Elliger, Wilhelm Rudolph, Hans Peter. Rüger, and G. E. Weil, eds. (1994); *Biblia Sacra Utriusque Testamenti Editio Hebraica Et Graeca;* Deutsche Bibelgesellschaft; . Stuttgart

Pickover, Clifford A. (2002); *The Zen of Magic Squares, Circles, and Stars: An Exhibition of Surprising Structures across Dimensions*. Princeton U. Press; Princeton, NJ

Plato. *Charmides, Alcibiades I and II, Hipparchus, The Lovers, Theages, Minos, Epinomis*; Trans. W. R. M. Lamb; Loeb Classical Library, Harvard U. Press; Cambridge; 1927

Plato. *The Republic: Books VI-X*. Trans. Paul Shorey; Loeb Classical Library; Harvard U. Press, 1994. Print. .

Sachs, Curt (2008); *The Rise of Music in the Ancient World, East and West*; Dover; New York

Scholem, Gershom Gerhard; (1987) *Kabbalah;*. Dover; New York

Tatlow, Ruth (1991); *Bach and the Riddle of the Number Alphabet*; Cambridge University Press; Cambridge

Trumble, William, and Lesley Brown, eds. (2002); *The Shorter Oxford English Dictionary*. Oxford: Oxford U. Press

Williams, Robert (1979) *The Geometrical Foundation of Natural Structure: A Source Book of Design*; Dover

www.ingramcontent.com/pod-product-compliance
Lightning Source LLC
Chambersburg PA
CBHW071753020426
42331CB00008B/2306